LEVEL 1 SCIENCE

LET'S READ AND FIND OUT

SUPER MARSUPIALS
KANGAROOS, KOALAS, WOMBATS, AND MORE

BY KATHARINE KENAH · ILLUSTRATED BY STEPHANIE FIZER COLEMAN

HARPER

An Imprint of HarperCollinsPublishers

Special thanks to Kathy Russell, General Curator, Santa Fe College Teaching Zoo,
Species Survival Plan - Program Coordinator for Matschie's Tree Kangaroo,
and Jacque Blessington, Survival Plan - Program Advisor for Matschie's Tree Kangaroo,
Senior Recreation Director/Naturalist.

We'd also like to thank Dr. Allan Burbidge, Principal Research Scientist,
Department of Biodiversity, Conservation and Attractions, Western Australia.

The Let's-Read-and-Find-Out Science book series was originated by Dr. Franklyn M. Branley, Astronomer Emeritus and former Chairman of the American Museum of Natural History–Hayden Planetarium, and was formerly co-edited by him and Dr. Roma Gans, Professor Emeritus of Childhood Education, Teachers College, Columbia University. Text and illustrations for each of the books in the series are checked for accuracy by an expert in the relevant field. For more information about Let's-Read-and-Find-Out Science books, write to HarperCollins Children's Books, 195 Broadway, New York, NY 10007, or visit our website at www.letsreadandfindout.com.

Let's Read-and-Find-Out Science® is a trademark of HarperCollins Publishers.

Library of Congress Cataloging-in-Publication Data

Names: Kenah, Katharine, author. | Coleman, Stephanie Fizer, illustrator.
Title: Super marsupials : kangaroos, koalas, wombats, and more / by Katharine Kenah ; illustrated by Stephanie Fizer Coleman.
Other titles: Let's-read-and-find-out science. Stage 1.
Description: First edition. | New York, NY : HarperCollins Children's Books, [2019] |
Series: Let's-Read-and-Find-Out Science Level 1 | Audience: Ages 4–8. | Audience: K to grade 3.
Identifiers: LCCN 2018025422| ISBN 978-0-06-249541-9 (hardback) | ISBN 978-0-06-249529-7 (pbk.)
Subjects: LCSH: Marsupials—Juvenile literature.
Classification: LCC QL737.M3 K46 2019 | DDC 599.2—dc23 LC record available at https://lccn.loc.gov/2018025422

The artist used Procreate and Photoshop to create the digital illustrations for this book.
Typography by Erica De Chavez and Honee Jang
19 20 21 22 23 SCP 10 9 8 7 6 5 4 3 2 1
❖
First Edition

To all the super animals around the world—K.K.
For Seth, always—S.F.C.

People keep their babies in cribs. Birds keep their babies in nests. Bears keep their cubs in caves. Some animals keep their babies in pouches. A **pouch** is a soft, furry pocket on the front of the mother's body.

Animals with babies in pouches are called **marsupials**.

There are over three hundred kinds of marsupials. Most of them live in **Australia**. But marsupials are not all the same.

Some fly like a kite.

Some move as fast as a car.

Some scream and jump to protect their food.

Some sleep all day.

Some are good climbers.

Some dig homes deep underground.

And others dangle upside down.

Marsupials are different from each other, but when they are first born there are four things marsupial babies all have in common:

- They are born pink and shiny and have no fur.
- They are as tiny as beans.
- They can't see or hear yet.
- They have no back legs.

All marsupial babies are called **joeys**.

KANGAROOS

Inside their mothers' pouches, **kangaroo** joeys stay safe and warm and fed for months.

While the babies are drinking their mothers' milk, their bodies are growing bigger . . .

13

and **bigger**.

When a joey can see and hear, has back legs and fur, and knows how to eat grass, it is ready to leave its mother's pouch.

Male kangaroos are called **boomers**.

Female kangaroos are called **flyers**.

Young kangaroos stay close to their mothers for a long time while they learn how to live on their own.

If a kangaroo joey is scared, it dives back into its mother's pouch and does a somersault to turn upright!

17

Kangaroos have super hearing! They turn their ears backward and forward so they can hear sounds all around them.

Kangaroos have sensitive noses. They live in big groups called **mobs**. When two kangaroos meet, they sniff each other's noses. That way they can tell if they belong to the same mob or if they are strangers!

Kangaroos' long eyelashes protect their eyes from bright sun, hot air, and dust.

Kangaroos can keep their eyes open to watch their joeys and look out for danger. If a kangaroo sees danger coming, it jumps up and down to warn other members of its mob.

Kangaroos have long tails that are strong enough to support them like chairs.

Sometimes male kangaroos box each other. They lean back and balance on their tails so they can kick with their back feet.

Kangaroos hop because their back legs always move together. But they can't hop backward. Their tails are in the way!

When kangaroos are moving fast, they bounce like rubber balls. Kangaroos get new energy with every bounce.

Not all kangaroos hop and live on the ground. Some kangaroos have treetop views!

TREE KANGAROOS

Tree kangaroos are cousins to kangaroos that live on the ground, but these cousins live mostly in trees. Tree kangaroos' front legs are longer than their back legs, and they can move their back legs one at a time.

Tree kangaroos' paws have rough pads and strong, curved claws. These features make tree kangaroos excellent climbers.

Tree kangaroos climb trees from branch to branch. They walk along one branch, then reach out to move to the next one. If a branch is too small or weak, they find a different way up the tree. A tree kangaroo can drop sixty feet to the ground without being hurt!

KOALAS

Koalas are called koala bears. They look like stuffed animals, with their soft bodies and big fluffy ears. But koalas are not bears. They are marsupials.

Koalas are **nocturnal**, which means they sleep during the day and search for food at night. Koalas spend most of each day sleeping in **eucalyptus** trees.

24

Eucalyptus leaves are poisonous to some animals and smell like cough drops. But they are koalas' favorite food. Koalas eat so many eucalyptus leaves, they smell like them!

DID YOU KNOW?

Koalas have five toes on their front paws. Their toe prints look just like human fingerprints.

When a koala baby is too big to fit in its mother's pouch, it rides on her back.

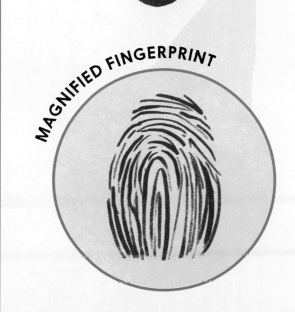

MAGNIFIED FINGERPRINT

WOMBATS

Wombats are like furry bulldozers. They have thick, strong bodies and dig so much, their pouches face backward. That way their babies don't get covered with dirt.

DID YOU KNOW?

Wombats' teeth grow continuously. They get worn down by eating tough grass.

Wombats live in homes called **burrows**. Their burrows are so deep underground, they are fireproof. Burrows connected by tunnels are called **warrens**. A wombat usually lives alone in its burrow, unless it is sharing the burrow with its baby.

Wombats have such big, tough rear ends that if a wombat is being chased, it dives into its tunnel and blocks the opening with its rear end!

TASMANIAN DEVILS

Tasmanian devils live on an Australian island called Tasmania.
They are fierce, meat-eating marsupials, about the size of a small dog.

But Tasmanian devils are not good hunters. They go out at night
in search of small animals that have been killed by other animals.

Tasmanian devils do not like to share their food. They scream and hiss and jump and growl to scare off other animals. Their ears turn bright red. Most of all they try to look big!

Tasmanian devils do this by jumping from side to side and showing their teeth to their enemies. They do this over and over so fast, it looks like they are spinning in circles.

Not all marsupials hop or spin. Some marsupials fly!

29

SUGAR GLIDERS

What is that flying across the sky? Is it a kite or a flying squirrel? No, it is a **sugar glider**!

Sugar gliders are small nocturnal marsupials with a fondness for sweet food. They like nectar from flowers and sap from trees. To get at the sap, they tear off pieces of bark and bite into a tree.

Sugar gliders have thin, furry folds of skin on both sides of their bodies. These stretch from their hands to their feet.

When a sugar glider leaps from a tree with its arms and legs spread wide, these folds act like airplane wings and keep the glider up in the air. Sugar gliders can control where they are going by moving their front legs up and down.

31

OPOSSUMS

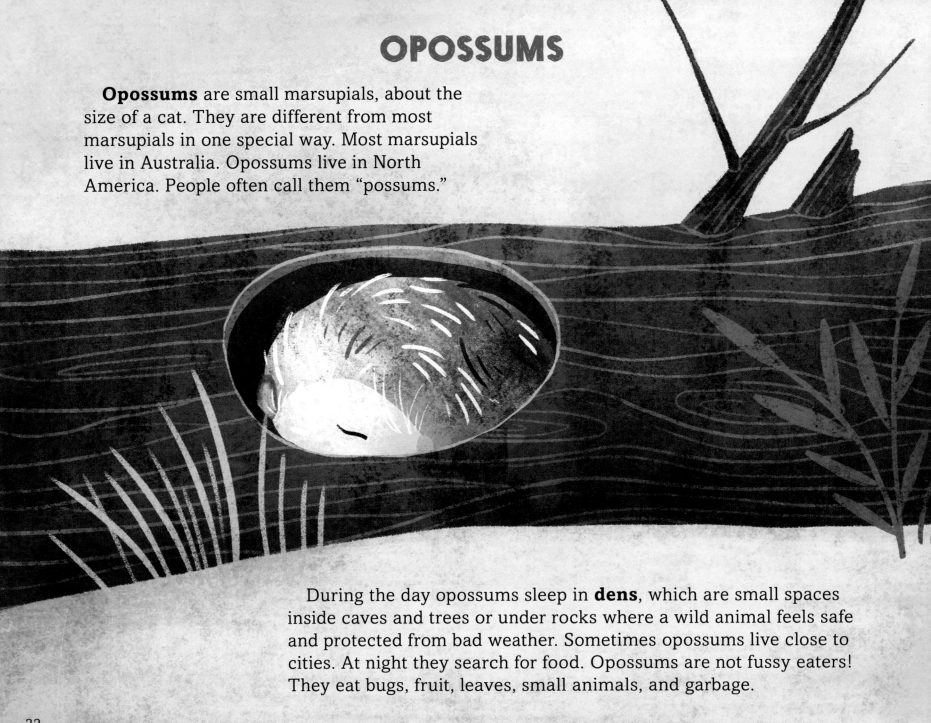

Opossums are small marsupials, about the size of a cat. They are different from most marsupials in one special way. Most marsupials live in Australia. Opossums live in North America. People often call them "possums."

During the day opossums sleep in **dens**, which are small spaces inside caves and trees or under rocks where a wild animal feels safe and protected from bad weather. Sometimes opossums live close to cities. At night they search for food. Opossums are not fussy eaters! They eat bugs, fruit, leaves, small animals, and garbage.

A female opossum can have thirteen babies in her pouch at once. When the babies are big enough to leave her pouch, they climb onto her back and ride there together for weeks.

Opossums have **prehensile** tails, which means they use them to hold on to things. Their tails have no fur and can curl around tree branches. That is how opossums can dangle upside down.

DID YOU KNOW?

When an opossum is scared, it plays dead. It falls onto its side and doesn't move until it feels safe again.

Marsupials look different, they live in different places, and they eat different things. But marsupials *all* work hard to keep their babies safe!

34

FIND OUT MORE

Joey Day

Marsupials take good care of their tiny babies. Joeys stay safe and warm and fed in their mothers' pouches until they are ready to live on their own. Some joeys stay in pouches for weeks, others for months! What would it be like to have a joey with you *all* the time?

Materials:

- Favorite stuffed animal (or something else special and nonbreakable)
- Backpack

Put a stuffed animal in your backpack. Wear your backpack on your *front*. Keep your joey in your "pouch" all morning, all afternoon, or all day.

Take good care of your joey while you are inside, outside, eating, on the bus, doing homework, whatever you are doing . . . wherever you are.

What would it be like to have the responsibility of taking care of a joey for months and keeping it safe while it grows? How would that change your life?

GLOSSARY

AUSTRALIA: A large island continent in the southern hemisphere. It is home to the most marsupials in the world.

BOOMER: A male kangaroo

BURROW: A home animals dig deep in the ground

DEN: A small space inside a cave or under rocks and trees where a wild animal goes to stay safe and protected

EUCALYPTUS: A kind of tree with long, tough leaves

FLYER: A female kangaroo

JOEY: A marsupial baby

KANGAROO: A large plant-eating marsupial. A kangaroo's hind legs are bigger than its front legs. A kangaroo moves by hopping and has a strong tail.

KOALA: A small marsupial that sleeps in eucalyptus trees during the day and eats eucalyptus leaves. A koala hunts for food at night.

MARSUPIAL: An animal that carries its underdeveloped baby in a pouch while the baby grows bigger. Most live in Australia.

MOB: A large group of kangaroos living together

NOCTURNAL: Active at night. Nocturnal animals sleep during the day and search for food at night.

OPOSSUM: A small nocturnal marsupial that lives in North America

POUCH: A soft, furry pocket on a mother marsupial's body, where babies stay safe and warm and fed until they grow big enough to live on their own

PREHENSILE: Adapted for holding on to things, especially by wrapping around an object. Opossums hold on to tree branches with their prehensile tails.

SUGAR GLIDER: A marsupial with folds of skin on both sides of its body that hold the glider up when it jumps from trees

TASMANIAN DEVIL: A fierce, meat-eating marsupial, with a very strong bite. A Tasmanian devil jumps quickly from side to side to look bigger.

TREE KANGAROO: A kind of kangaroo that lives in trees. A tree kangaroo can move its back legs separately and is an excellent climber.

WARREN: Animal burrows connected by tunnels

WOMBAT: A wide, strong marsupial with a pouch that faces backward

MARSUPIALS

KANGAROO

OPOSSUM

TREE KANGAROO

SUGAR GLIDER

KOALA

TASMANIAN DEVIL

WOMBAT

Be sure to look for all of these books in the **Let's-Read-and-Find-Out Science** series: